I FIT OUT:
Chronicles of an Unapologetic Misfit

AMBER J.

Copyright © 2019 Amber Jefferson

All rights reserved. No part of this publication may be reproduced, distributed, or transmitted in any form or by any means, including photocopying, recording, or other electronic or mechanical methods, without the prior written permission of the Publisher, except in the case of brief quotations embodied in critical reviews and certain other noncommercial uses permitted by copyright law. For permission requests, write to the author, addressed "Attention: Permissions Coordinator," at the address below.

Amber J.
Liberated.s.m@gmail.com
www.theliberatedsoulmovement.com

ISBN-13: 978-0-578-58897-1

Publishing Coordination & Cover Design By ThriveHer Publishing House visit us at www.rrebirthingcenter.com

Table of Contents

Self- Identity

Visibly Invisible 3
I Won't Back Down 6
A Cage Called Perfection 9
Birth of a Queen 11
Beauty for Ashes 13
Gypsy Queen 15
Unapologetic 17
Ode to the Queen 19
I Fit Out 22
Crisis of Identity 24

Relationship Identity

A Heart's Truth 29
New Love 31
Fire Dancer 33
Dragon Slayer 37
Flip a Coin 40
Silent Flight 42
The Price of the Covering 45

Healing Identity

Questions	51
Elemental Magic	54
Spirit Warrior	56
The Last Goodbye	58
Triggers	60
Saint & Sinner	63
Stolen Power	65
Tapped Out	67
Pulse Check	69
Beyond the Mask	71
Peanut Gallery Takedown	73
Love Me Gently	76
End of the Line	79

Dedication

This book is dedicated to the weirdos, the misfits, and the first-class non-conformists. May this creative outpour remind you that you are seen, your experience is valid, and your life is valuable.

To my number 1 misfit, my baby girl, you kept me pushing forward when I was at my lowest and emptiest.

To God, thank you for the privilege to write the truth and use it to impact others.

"You're entirely bonkers. But I'll tell you a secret, all the best people are."

~ Alice in Wonderland

Self- Identity

*You are the only you in existence.
That matters.*

Visibly Invisible

Just keep smiling.

If I don't tell them they're hurting me, then maybe they'll stay.

A twisted mentality rooted in the gaps of my own emotional needs.

Fully believing that if I never showed that I had needs, maybe they'd never leave.

Constantly over-performing so they'd see me as worthy; ignoring that I was at their mercy.

Never setting a boundary, because what were my needs compared to theirs?

Sacrificing my dignity and self-respect for their affection.

But truly seeking a space where reciprocity is key.

Where I can be accepted with all of my emotional needs.

Learning healthy boundaries and what it takes for me to be happy with me.

No longer visibly invisible.

But present and visible for all to see.

I am a whole me regardless of them.

I Won't Back Down

Did it make you feel better when I hid from you?

Cowering in my internal shell waiting for your retreat.

Did I make you feel powerful?

Quickly backing down so attacks would cease.

Swearing that there was no reason for you to chase me.

Wondering what it was you saw when you would see me.

I didn't have an answer.

I didn't have a clue.

Because I couldn't even to my own self be true.

So I sat at my wits end.

Wishing for it all to stop.

Wondering what would happen with one short drop.

But I pulled myself back.

I held myself firm.

Talked to my life about how it could turn.

Around.

So day by day.

I walk towards the light within

Knowing the only one in control of me is me.

*If they understood your tears,
they'd never question your desire
to see them smile.*

A Cage Called Perfection

If I show you my scars, will you still think I'm beautiful?

Worthy of the praise and adoration you so often bestow

I've been broken and abused.

Am I still perfect to you?

The remnants of anxieties and insecurities weave a tapestry across my mind.

Can you still love me?

Will you allow me to be me and you to be you imperfections and all?

I'm hoping.

Be your own kind of amazing instead of everyone else's kind of normal.

Birth of a Queen

She broke the mold you made for her.

She kicked your too-small box to the curb.

And laughed at your limited imagination.

You only saw a candle, but she was the true flame.

You wanted to contain her spirit, but she is the gypsy whose soul runs free.

You felt her warm breeze not realizing she was the storm on the horizon.

And you were mesmerized.

The lightning that was her smile bright and dazzling.

The breeze that was her touch softly caressing.

And the thunder that was her sex intense and surrounding.

I will not hide my scars and flaws behind a mask. I will wear them as a badge of pride.

Beauty for Ashes

I studied her.

The serene with otherworldly peace.

She transcended the realm of logic.

Scars turned to stars and beauty given for ashes.

My reflection.

The healing process made visible in the mirror.

*I am not meant to be tamed
or controlled simply loved and
embraced as I am.*

Gypsy Queen

And she loved herself more than she ever thought possible.

The gypsy Queen who dances to beat of her own drum.

She is wild n free exactly as her creator intended her to be.

Embracing her mind, her thighs, her ideas, and eyes.

Looking towards the horizon.

The future that had no limit, wonders that never cease, and dreams that know no boundaries.

She is an unstoppable force.

Spinning like a hurricane, dropping rain that sprouts flowers and knowledge that grows generations.

She is the gypsy queen there are no mountains she can't climb nor oceans she can't cross.

Dance with her if you dare.

For her magic is not for the faint of heart.

*I move differently
and I'm good with that.*

Unapologetic

For the first time, I loved me differently.

Looking past perceived scars, flaws, and past wrongs.

Seeing the true beauty within my courage, compassion, and determination

And I smiled.

No longer seeking external validation and attention from others.

I basked in the revelry of being unapologetically me.

*I will not limit myself
to fit society's labels.*

Ode to the Queen

Gypsy rebel with the heart of gold.

The one created to break the mold.

Now crown could define her and she certainly didn't need it to signify her as royal. She was royal by design.

An awakened soul with the dust of the stars in her eyes and the light of the sun in her smile.

The first of her kind and the blueprint all others would follow.

A diamond shining in the deepest mine.

A pearl in the deepest sea.

She was royal without apology.

And no man could shackle her to his ideology.

For she is storm and fire burning away your every facade and cleansing you with purifying rain.

Truly wild n free as her creator meant her to be.

This is my ode to the queen who's hair defies gravity, skin declares royalty, and wisdom will demand your loyalty.

*I am dope without Apology
or Explanation.*

I Fit Out

I stopped trying to be who they wanted me to be.

Mentally bound in chains that destroyed me internally.

Societal expectations that justified the status quo,

But contorted me at the root of my soul.

Creating anxieties and insecurities continuously telling me that I'd never be free.

Until the day I realized my freedom is on me.

Owing no apologies or explanations for my authenticity or the creativity that flows through me.

I choose every day to bask in my truth.

Knowing that I'll never be chained again.

*I haven't changed.
I'm just being me louder.*

Crisis of Identity

Their first mistake was thinking their narrow vision of me was all there was to me.

My first mistake was believing them.

Breaking off pieces of me to fit the box they'd created for me.

Buffing and blending until my perceived personality became their reality losing the truth of my identity in the process.

Thinking conformity was the only way to gain acceptance.

A social chameleon constantly hiding in plain sight.

Quivering at the thought of being unmasked.

But secretly straining against the confinement of the four walls around me.

Yearning to break free.

*"I wasn't born to belong to anyone.
I was born to share myself with
someone who shares an equal part
of themselves with me."*

~ Unknown

Relationship Identity

The journey begins with a single Yes.

A Heart's Truth

And if I touch your heart would you let me stay there?

Steadily remove the bricks and lay your soul bare.

I know this thing between us is scary, but if you'll trust me and I trust you

I think our hearts will be made new.

Repairing the damage from the one who wasn't true.

Who couldn't appreciate and or reciprocate the love that we tried to cultivate.

So when I touch your heart will you let me stay?

Keep your fear of love at bay.

Remind you that your days of wishing and hoping have passed away because the foundation we're laying is for a lifetime.

I'm too busy loving myself to try to be someone else.

New Love

And I loved to watch him sleep,

When stress eased and peace took over.

I caressed his brow and drifted.

Am I dreaming?

Is this really love that I'm feeling?

This flutter in my chest,

Sublime contentment and joy unimaginable.

I never thought I'd get back to this place, but as I lay here and look at this man

My heart swells.

It's love personified.

We grow as we move and move as we grow.

Towards dreams unfathomable and depths unmeasurable.

Our love is a love for the books.

The kind we dream of telling our children of.

In hopes that they would grow in love too.

Leave your wall up, but lower your drawbridge when you're talking to me.

Fire Dancer

But how can you hide from her?

You brought yourself into her light.

Unable to resist

A gravitational pull that caused your world to shift

The vulnerability was new to you, but your heart won't quit.

Your ego resisted, but your mind said submit.

And when your eyes locked with hers,

Your world melted away.

And she jolted you awake.

She put the defibrillator to your chest and shocked your heart awake.

Numbness

Was all you'd known

You'd clung to it like a cloak.

Seeking the comfort of it's emotionless void.

Avoiding the vulnerabilities and insecurities he carried in his skin

Hoping no one would see the truth he carried deep within.

Until she came

Flooding your world with her dazzling light

Her love coursed through your veins like wild fire

Burning down your fears and your doubts and rebuilding you with hope.

So, you stood in her fire and you added gasoline

You danced a dance of revelry

In awe of her intensity

Unafraid of the flames lapping at your skin

You laughed in the face of danger.

Disregarding the possibility of being consumed by her ferocity,

You bowed at the thrown of the queen.

Hoping to be singed by her kiss and devoured by her flames

You stood with longing

Hoping for a sample of her nectar

Unconcerned with the price she'd demand you pay

For you'd pay it willingly, joyfully for all eternity.

*Me loving me has nothing
to do with you.*

Dragon Slayer

So I met this guy one time,

He was everything.

Dazzling smile.

Broad shoulders.

Just Everything.

He was charismatic,

And said all the right things.

But I was too naive to see the truth.

That he was just a shell.

But still, I fell.

Every second of every day.

Further,

Deeper,

And common sense was nowhere in sight.

Until one day I found myself

Empty

And the woman I used to be was nowhere in sight.

And I had no clue where to find her.

So I journeyed, I walked, and I ran.

Starving for my own truth.

Begging for a glimpse of the woman I used to be.

Until one day,

I met a dragon slayer.

Bold and fierce.

Her armor, the lies people told about her.

Her shield was the truth that lies deep within.

Her sword, her dreams for the future.

She took my hand and told me

To get up and fight.

I looked in her eye,

And she looked so familiar.

Then I realized, that she was me.

*Freedom is knowing their box
ain't for you.*

Flip a Coin

We were two sides to the same coin.

Eerily similar yet astoundingly different.

I felt while you thought.

Your logic to my intuition.

Differences that create balance or differences that create division.

I couldn't tell.

I was obsessed.

I fell under your spell.

Craving your intellect, your zeal, and the way you made me feel.

Not caring for the fact we were on two different paths.

Until one became two again.

Fractured.

Broken.

Trying to figure out how to reassemble the broken pieces I find myself in.

I am powerful because of my experiences.

Silent Flight

The silence was deafening, but the eyes don't lie.

Rage rolled off her like tidal waves crashing at sea.

A forced silence caused taut muscles and choked back words cuz accountability was his enemy which made silence her safety.

While she battled his ego, his issues, and his hidden insecurities.

He evaded the problem, accused falsely, and blustered profusely.

Until her anger turned to distance as arguments increased.

And she searched for a way out to put her mind at ease

Gradually building an exit strategy to escape with sanity knowing her entire future was at stake.

Quietly checking calendars and rates until stars aligned and told her fate.

Silently fleeing with all belongings in tow.

Moving forward to see what her life had in store.

Choosing peace over materialistic comfort.

Embracing an unknown that was all her own.

*I am not required to prioritize
another's comfort over my own dignity
or self-respect.*

The Price of the Covering

I stopped sacrificing myself for your comfort.

Giving what I didn't have so you wouldn't feel loss.

Praying for you when I needed someone to cover me too.

Allowing you space in my tranquility, but receiving only turbulence in exchange.

Quietly giving the best of me while receiving the worst of you.

You were an emotional vampire.

Perpetually sucking me to within inches of my life only to allow me to recover so you could feed again.

And I tried to ignore my intuition.

Wanting to believe that you were a better you that your pattern showed to be true.

Foolishly thinking that I needed we more than I needed me.

But I know better now.

"You've outgrown the old you. You're uncomfortable because your old life doesn't fit anymore."

~ Leighann Heil

Healing Identity

I met my soul, so I could meet myself authentically.

Questions

I'm really startin to wonder did we box God in?

Limiting the capacity of who God is with our made up religions.

I'm just askin.

That book written in the tongues of men.

Is that really all God is or did too many men put their finger in the pie?

For narrow is the way as the good book says, but did God really define what narrow is, or did men's fears do that for us?

Because I've seen more of God in the Atheist, the Muslim, and the homosexual than the believer.

So did we box God in?

Limit Him with sexism and the constructs of men.

Overlay Him with patriarchy to limit the possibilities of women and men who don't fit in.

I'm just askin.

Cuz the religion you teachin and the God I keep meetin don't match.

So I really have to wonder who you're truly servin.

The God who created the heavens and everything below or yourself in disguise.

I cannot be content being mediocre when I know greatness is in me.

Elemental Magic

The sun kissed me and told me to glow. Wrapped me in her rays til she flowed through my soul.

The water buried me. Crushed me in her depths til I was born anew, eroding life's toxic layers until my true hues showed through.

The wind shifted me, tossed me to and fro blowing me to destinations unknown yet pointing me to true North

The Earth covered me, planted me in darkness til roots ran deep, nurtured me till I could stand on my own feet.

The four elements working in harmony to create the me the world needs.

*I live for the fire that burns in me
while doing the things I believe in.*

Spirit Warrior

The most impregnable towers still need maintenance.

The thickest walls still get patched,

And the strongest warriors still need time to rest.

Time to replenish.

Time to restore.

The sighs of relief rise from their heavily burdened souls.

Souls accustomed carrying the woes of the world.

Holding space for the weary and broken,

Uplifting the lost and despondent.

They are Spirit Warriors fighting unseen battles and winning unknown wars.

Wars against depression, anxieties, and demons of the night

Warring to make the internally bound free.

I find my freedom in wholly embracing myself.

The Last Goodbye

I'm sorry but you have to die.

Looking in the mirror seeing my old self reflected back at me.

Old mentalities and philosophies stifle the new me coming forward.

Unhealed triggers work to stay in the shadows continually sabotaging chances to heal.

My insecurities and self-doubt tag team crafting smoke and mirror illusions clouding judgment and identity.

All coming together to form the perfect chokehold around the new me I'm birthing.

Ready to smother her before she draws breath.

I'm no longer sorry you have to die.

Pruned like dead branches off a budding tree.

I'm no longer sorry you have to die.

The new me is calling and this time I'm ready to pick up.

I am only responsible for the outcome of my life.

Triggers

Triggers.

We all have them.

Healing wounds from past trauma suddenly irritated by familiar experience.

Verbal disagreements giving deja vu' of prior abuse.

Walling people out for fear of repeating past hurts

Lashing out at the new because the old wasn't true

Mentally shutting down to avoid perceived future pain.

Yearning for deep love, though fearful of the repercussion of letting go of control.

And at the root of it all,

Fear.

Fear of suppressed memories resurrected from a long-buried past.

Pain.

Pain deeply rooted refusing to be dug up.

But I came with a shovel, machete, and axe and hacked until healing came and I refuse to turn back.

I accept there is darkness and light in everything, even in me.

Saint & Sinner

I told myself I wasn't who they thought I was.

But, maybe I am.

Not the heroine but the villain.

A master magician creating illusions in the minds of all.

Saint turned sinner not minding the fall.

I went searching for an angel and the devil came to call.

Asking who I would decide to be.

The fake, the fraud, the con artist or the healer, the lover, and the friend.

So I took a look inside myself where I'd put my heart upon the shelf and wondered

When will I stop pretending at who they want me to be and become who I know I am.

I am letting go of who they said I was and embracing all that I am.

Stolen Power

It said I was unlovable,

Undeserving,

And Unworthy.

The poisonous voice inhabiting the gray matter between my ears.

Shame.

It was my jailor and constant companion.

Giving no quarter or hope of redemption.

Overshadowing every step forward till it became steps backward.

Silencing my story dead in its tracks.

Til forgiveness met shame and shut down its lies.

Unlocked my jail and called me outside.

So now here I stand in the light of the sun.

Joy overwhelming and peace overflowing.

Knowing there's nowhere my story won't run.

The sky is not my limit.

Tapped Out

One wasn't enough.

It should've been.

But the second I got my hands on the one,

I needed another.

Insatiable.

A hole I couldn't quite fill.

Constantly demanding.

A yearning I just couldn't satisfy and I didn't want to.

I had to have it all;

The highest position,

The biggest achievement,

The newest trinket.

Consuming til there was no more only to find I was the one being consumed all along.

My fears do not control my future.

Pulse Check

cold fingers dance up my spine.

Panic.

I'm running a race but there's no finish line.

And I can't stop these cold fingers cuttin off my air supply, so I choke.

I'm wounded, but there's no band aid for this hole.

The breakdown is imminent

It's always lurking and anticipating the widening chasm in my mind.

So don't disrupt my performance.

Don't disturb my mask.

You don't want to see the demons that stalk my daydreams.

*I am committed to loving
all parts of myself.*

Beyond the Mask

You wouldn't know her heartbreak from looking at her.

Pain hidden by smiles and contoured to perfection.

Quaking legs held steady by stilettos and pushed back shoulders.

High performing depression.

Applauded and celebrated publicly but breaking down internally.

Working with robotic precision to mask her dysfunction.

Praying for healing but so tired of kneeling.

Wondering if anyone will ever look behind the mask.

Cracked

Imperfect

Still worthy of love

Peanut Gallery Takedown

It could've been better.

The critique quickly comes.

Whispers across the mental distance.

Judging and finding the effort wanting.

A Samurai blade slicing and silencing what would've been a momentous occasion.

A relentless voice of perfection impossible to please.

And I swore I gave my best pouring hours, and minutes, and seconds into this moment.

But to no avail.

Perfection the cruel mistress.

Poking at unseen insecurities to create false realities that rob me of the joy of believing

I'm good enough.

And here I am constantly striving,

Constantly reaching.

For an unattainable standard

Causing crippling anxieties and halting all flows of creativity.

That's got me sittin up wondering if something's wrong with me

But my best is my best.

No matter what's said.

So perfection can shove it.

I'll just be excellent instead.

I am purposefully shaping my best life.

This piece is dedicated to every full-figured girl who ever sought protection and only received rejection.

Love Me Gently

They swear I couldn't need protection and I couldn't be soft on the inside,

Cuz girls like me don't need nobody.

We good all by ourselves.

And even though OutKast said, "Big girls need love too."

Y'all don't wanna hear allat.

So here I stand visibly invisible.

Hardly the one you call in the day, but always the one you come for at night.

Never the one you stand and defend, but always the one you need in the end.

Now, I'm so done with your foolishness and fuckery.

Wonderin why you won't choose me.

I refuse to allow your validation to be a prerequisite for my self-esteem or happiness

I choose me.

*You can't get where you're going
without going through where you are.*

End of the Line

It didn't start with me, but it ends here.

Corrupt cycles constantly eroding self-worth.

That turned into engrained trauma impacting and transforming generations to come.

Cuz it happened to Grandma and Momma

So why not me too?

Got me steady takin words thrown like stones mentally breakin my bones,

And I'm expected to accept his emotional absence cuz he won't heal.

I'm so drained.

Tired of fighting for what I knew I deserved

While working to preserve the generation arriving.

Knowing that in reality they thought I was crazy;

For refusing to tolerate what tore at my soul and

Balking at the ones who tried to control while tearing down strongholds meant to incapacitate the future.

But also meant to be a voice for those silenced in the past.

And I refused to believe that this was the family's true trajectory

Confined by the egos of men when dominion was meant to be birthed through us.

About the Author

Amber J. is a spoken word artist, misfit, and non-conventional coach who works to empower others to break free from societal chains, accept and identify who they truly are so they can walk in authenticity. Amber knows first-hand how it feels to fit out. She is a survivor of a ten year emotionally abusive relationship and has done extensive work to recover from anxiety, low self-esteem, and confidence.

She is the owner of The Liberated Soul Movement which is a brand that inspires others to be unapologetically unafraid to be themselves through various channels and events.

Amber is now a current resident of Atlanta, Georgia, and a divorced mom of one.

For more information on The Liberated Soul Movement check out www.theliberatedsoulmovement.com.